MUSICAL INSTRUMENTS

French Horns

Kimberly M. Hutmacher
and John Willis

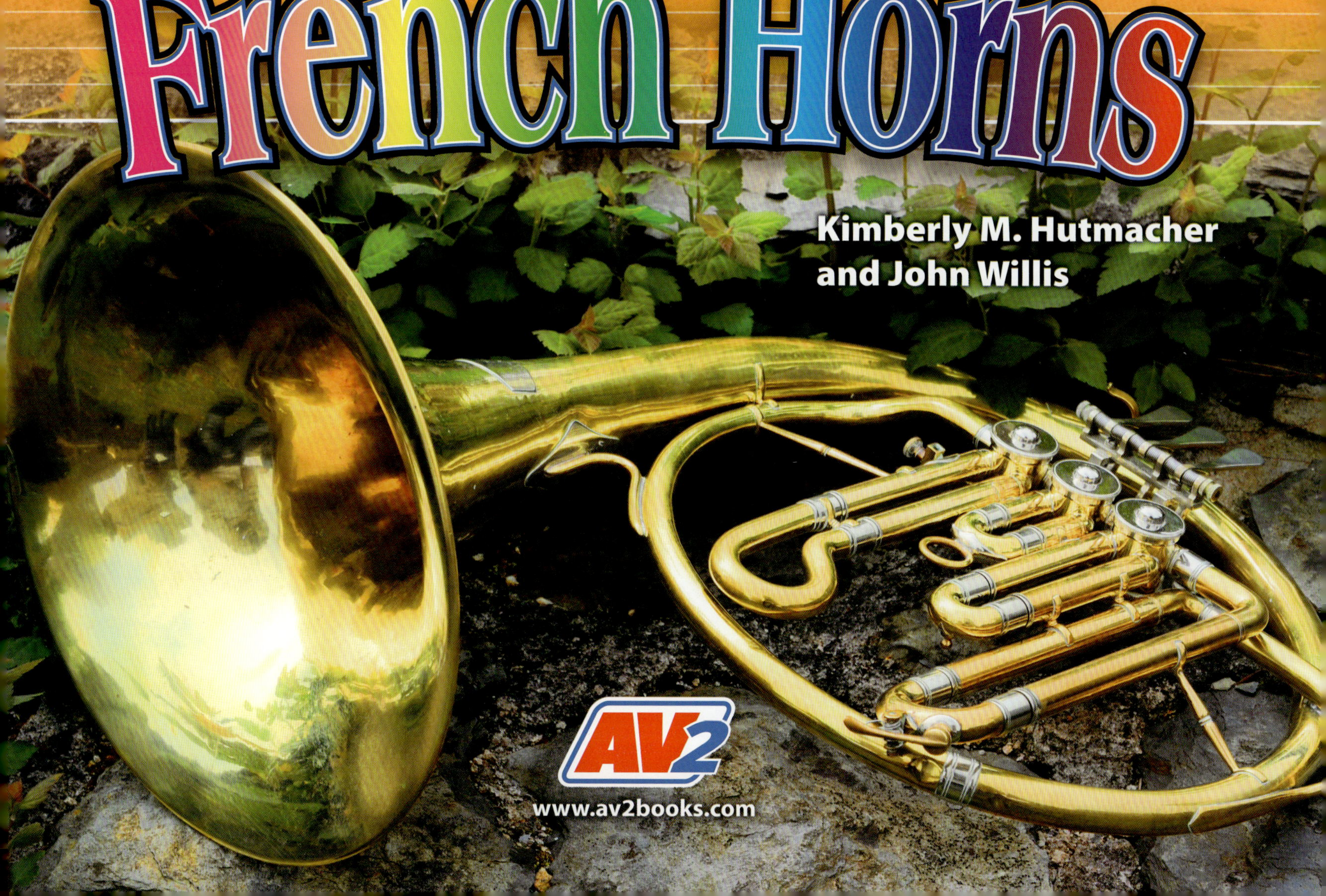

AV2
www.av2books.com

AV2

Step 1
Go to **www.av2books.com**

Step 2
Enter this unique code

YFRJPHY4G

Step 3
Explore your interactive eBook!

AV2 is optimized for use on any device

Your interactive eBook comes with...

Read

Audio
Listen to the entire book read aloud

Videos
Watch informative video clips

Weblinks
Gain additional information for research

Try This!
Complete activities and hands-on experiments

Key Words
Study vocabulary, and complete a matching word activity

Quizzes
Test your knowledge

Slideshows
View images and captions

View new titles and product videos at www.av2books.com

MUSICAL INSTRUMENTS

French Horns Contents

What is that sound?
Too-too-too-too-toooom!
It is time to play the
French horn.

The French horn is a musical instrument. It is made of tubes wound into a circle. A French horn has a bell shape on its end.

Players make a buzzing sound into the horn. Air moves through the tubes. Then, sound comes out of the bell.

People use 12 muscles to make the right mouth shape to play the French horn.

A French horn has buttons called valves. Players make different notes by pressing the valves.

Players put their right hand inside the bell. Moving their hand changes the sound.

Players can change the length of the tubes. A long tube makes a low sound. A short tube makes a high sound.

The tubing in a single horn can be almost 12 feet long. (3.6 meters)

The first horns were made from animal horns. The metal horns that became French horns were made about 400 years ago.

Horns did not have valves until the 19th century.

QVOD·COMES·ALBERT·ALSATIESIS
TVQ·DITAVIT·HEC·ACTA·SVT·ANN
O·M·C·XC·VIIII·

The French horn is played in classical music. It is also used in orchestras and military bands.

The French horn is a brass instrument. It is played with other brass instruments such as trumpets and tubas.

See what you have learned about French horns.

Which of these pictures does not show a French horn?

KEY WORDS

Research has shown that as much as 65 percent of all written material published in English is made up of 300 words. These 300 words cannot be taught using pictures or learned by sounding them out. They must be recognized by sight. This book contains 56 common sight words to help young readers improve their reading fluency and comprehension. This book also teaches young readers several important content words, such as proper nouns. These words are paired with pictures to aid in learning and improve understanding.

Page	Sight Words First Appearance
5	is, it, play, sound, that, the, time, to, what
6	a, end, has, into, its, made, of, on
9	air, comes, make, moves, out, people, right, then, through, use
10	by, different
13	changes, hand, put, their
15	almost, be, can, feet, high, in, long
16	about, animal, did, first, from, have, not, until, were, years
19	also, and
20	as, other, such, with

Page	Content Words First Appearance
5	French horn
6	circle, musical instrument, shape, tubes
9	muscles, players
10	buttons, notes, valves
16	metal horns
19	classical music, military bands, orchestras
20	trumpets, tubas

Published by AV2
350 5th Avenue, 59th Floor New York, NY 10118
Website: www.av2books.com

Library of Congress Cataloging-in-Publication Data

Names: Hutmacher, Kimberly, author.
Title: French horns / Kimberly M. Hutmacher and John Willis.
Description: New York : AV2, 2020. | Series: Musical instruments | Audience: Ages 4-6 | Audience: Grades K-1 |
Identifiers: LCCN 2019039060 (ebook) | LCCN 2019039061 (ebook) | ISBN 9781791116088 (library binding) |
ISBN 9781791116095 (paperback) | ISBN 9781791116101 | ISBN 9781791116118
Subjects: LCSH: Horn (Musical instrument)--Juvenile literature.

Classification: LCC ML955 .H89 2020 (print) | LCC ML955 (ebook) | DDC 788.9/419--dc23
LC record available at https://lccn.loc.gov/2019039060
LC ebook record available at https://lccn.loc.gov/2019039061

Printed in Guangzhou, China
1 2 3 4 5 6 7 8 9 0 24 23 22 21 20

022020
100919

Project Coordinator: John Willis Designer: Ana María Vidal

The publisher acknowledges Alamy, Getty Images, and iStock as the primary image suppliers for this title.